The Casual Quilter

6 STRESS-FREE PROJECTS

Robin Strobel

Martingale™
& COMPANY

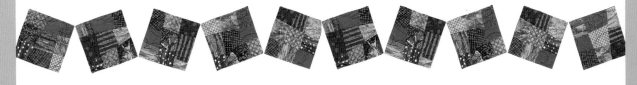

Credits

President • Nancy J. Martin
CEO • Daniel J. Martin
Publisher • Jane Hamada
Editorial Director • Mary V. Green
Managing Editor • Tina Cook
Technical Editor • Laurie Baker
Copy Editor • Allison A. Merrill
Design and Production Manager • Stan Green
Illustrator • Laurel Strand
Cover and Text Designer • Regina Girard
Photographer • Brent Kane

That Patchwork Place® is an imprint
of Martingale & Company™.

The Casual Quilter: 6 Stress-Free Projects
© 2002 by Robin Strobel

Martingale & Company
20205 144th Avenue NE
Woodinville, WA 98072-8478 USA
www.martingale-pub.com

Printed in China
07 06 05 04 03 02   8 7 6 5 4 3 2 1

Mission Statement

We are dedicated to providing quality products and service by working together to inspire creativity and to enrich the lives we touch.

Library of Congress Cataloging-in-Publication Data
Strobel, Robin.
  The casual quilter / Robin Strobel.
    p. cm.
  ISBN 1-56477-409-0
  1. Quilting–Patterns. 2. Patchwork–Patterns. I. Title.

TT835 .S745 2002
746.46–dc21   2001051419

Contents

Acknowledgments

It is not possible to thank everyone who is important to this book, but with delusions of grandeur and in the best tradition of the Academy Awards, I will try to do so and stay within my limit. First, my thanks to Janice Nelson, Shelley Nelson, and Sandy Bonsib, with whom I have quilted for many years. There is nothing so special as a group of friends coming together to quilt and to share joys, sorrows, families, illnesses, victories, and frustrations. You are my inspiration and support.

In addition, many, many thanks go to the following:

Lynn Serack, for teaching me the meaning of friendship;

Laurel Strand, illustrator extraordinaire, for believing in me;

Trish Carey, for being of generous heart and creative spirit;

Liz Warner, owner of QuiltWorks Northwest, for the opportunity to teach
amid a never ending parade of inspiring fabrics;

Patricia Rasmussen, for keeping me in balance;

Martingale & Company staff and friends;

My students, who teach me much more than I could ever teach them;

My father, Carl Strobel—you are in my heart forever.

The Casual Attitude

I think of casual quilts as quilts that are intended for use and abuse. They are without pretense or fancy trappings. Usually the patterns are simple and the piecing is quick. Often, a casual quilt is created as a gift for someone the quilter loves. One inexperienced quilter I know made a quilt for her first grandchild, and it was among the most beautiful quilts I have ever seen. The corners of the blocks did not quite match, the seams wobbled, and the quilting was nearly invisible (which was fortunate), but the love and joy and hope she had for her son's little daughter shone through every stitch. The grandmother was worried and embarrassed and afraid to give the quilt because of all of the "mistakes" in it. I was horrified. Would the child care that the corners were not perfect? Would she notice that the quilt was not precisely square? I imagined the little girl dragging the quilt around and cuddling in it, feeling her grandmother's love even when alone. Of course she had to have that quilt, inaccuracies and all!

I realized I had once been like the grandmother. I had never considered why I was making any given quilt, nor could I find any level of acceptance for errors or imperfections large or small. If it was not perfect, it was not good. Now I think about my reasons for making a quilt. If I want to enter the quilt in a show, it is worth my time and energy to tear out all mismatched points and seams until I can get the blasted pieces to look perfect. But if I want to give the quilt to my mother—who is eighty-six, has macular degeneration, and can't see a point no matter how perfect (and who would love the quilt even if she could see the imperfections)—I am more likely to let some mistakes remain in the quilt and concentrate on finishing it within her lifetime.

At this point in my quilting career, when I make a casual quilt, I am not attempting to create a major opus in three layers. I anticipate that the quilt will

accompany people I care about to the beach, a picnic, or a soccer game. The quilt will be rolled in on the grass or left out on a hammock in the rain. It will have cat hair and tears shed on it and crackers and sticky stuff ground into the fibers. I hope my casual quilt will be used until the colors fade and the fabrics fray, and then be given to the dog to sleep on. With this outlook, why should I fret over every corner, point, and seam? I believe every quilter needs to find tolerance for imperfections and not let the opinions of others keep him or her from enjoying and sharing creations.

Too often tragedy strikes swiftly, leaving little time to prepare. Giving a quilt is a priceless way to reach out and show you care. In many cases, making the quilt as quickly as possible is essential. Choose fabrics that will bring joy and comfort to the recipient and to you. Fun prints with puppies, kittens, trucks, or houses are more important in a child's quilt than a perfectly matched color scheme. Sew with hopes and memories. Give with love. Perfection is not required.

Casual Basics

Here are just a few ideas and techniques that work well for me. If you have never made a quilt, you will want to supplement this book. Take classes, go to guild meetings, frequent a quilt store, and read lots and lots of books. Explore the many techniques and tools that make quilting quicker, easier, and more fun. Discover what works for you.

Choosing Fabrics

"If you like it, it works."

The Casual Quilter

I have studied color theory, color use in quilts, fabric dyeing, and graphic design, and believe in three main rules for choosing fabrics.

1. *You can use any colors you like together.* No matter what the combination of colors, somewhere it's considered a scheme and has a big, fancy name. If you like it, it works.

2. Block patterns depend more on value, which is the relative lightness or darkness of the fabrics, than on colors. One of the rules of "good" design is that a design should contain a wide range of values from light to dark, yet sometimes this full range of value looks too harsh in a quilt. *If you like the values you have chosen, it works.*

3. *Colors do not have to match perfectly.* Quilts often look better if the hues in the different fabrics are not identical. For example, look at the floral print in the photo above right; it mixes purple with medium and light blues. Instead of choosing fabrics with identical purples and blues, like those shown to the lower right of the floral fabric, I like to use fabrics with slightly stronger colors, like those to the upper left of the floral fabric. You may prefer the matching group, or you may want to push the colors even further from the original. We all have our own color comfort zone. It is OK to stay within yours, or to try something different. If you don't like the result, give the quilt to charity.

Fabrics on the upper left enhance, rather than exactly match, the colors in the floral print. Fabrics on the lower right match the floral print perhaps too well.

Cutting

"If you are going to be accurate, this is the place for it."

The Casual Quilter

I believe in putting my effort into those things that will make quilting easier in the long run and that will show on the finished quilt. What is important varies from pattern to pattern, but the most critical step is usually measuring and cutting the initial pieces exactly the recommended size. Inaccuracy in cutting will haunt you throughout the entire project. Sewing with a perfect ¼" seam won't help if the pieces were not cut exactly right. Take the time to cut accurately. It makes sewing the quilt a lot quicker and easier.

Many quilters like to use the lines on the cutting mat to measure strips and pieces. Although I am a firm believer in rotary cutting, I am incapable of cutting accurately using these lines. If you find that your strips and pieces are not accurate, try the following two-ruler approach. You will need a rotary mat, rotary cutter, and two rulers. I prefer a 6" x 24" ruler for cutting and a 6" x 12" ruler for measuring, although the measuring ruler can be any size you have on hand.

1. Iron all of the fabrics that will be used in the quilt. Fold each one wrong sides together with the selvage edges aligned. If the fabric has been cut off-grain, shift the selvage edges in opposite directions until the wrinkles disappear. Lay the fabric on the rotary mat with the folded edge toward you.

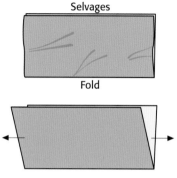

Selvages

Fold

Shift until wrinkles disappear.

2. If you are cutting strips of identical width from several fabrics, layer them, slightly offsetting the folded edges. Depending on your skill level and the sharpness of your rotary cutter, you can layer up to six fabrics and still make perfect cuts.

3. Straighten one end of the fabric by aligning a line on the 6" x 24" ruler with the folded edge of the fabric. Position the ruler only as far in from the raw edges as needed to cut through all layers of fabric. Cut along the long edge of the ruler. Be certain all layers have a clean, straight edge.

4. Use the measuring ruler to measure a strip of the appropriate width from the straightened edge. Place the 6" x 24" ruler against the edge of the measuring ruler. If your measuring ruler is shorter than the width of the folded fabric, slide it up and down the 6" x 24" ruler to be certain the strip you cut measures the same at every point. Set the measuring ruler aside and cut along the 6" x 24" ruler's edge.

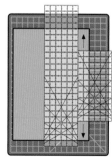

Slide measuring ruler to check accuracy.

Casual Tip

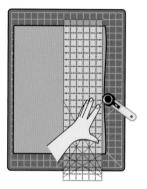

I use an inchworm approach to cutting. I start with my hand near the base of the ruler and cut to a height just above my fingertips. Then, without moving the cutter or ruler, I bring the thumb on the hand bracing the ruler up to just below my fingers, then extend my fingers to brace the top half of the ruler. I then cut the remainder of the strip.

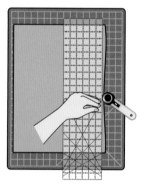

Pause cutting level with tips of fingers, but do not lift cutter from fabric.

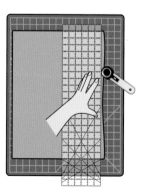

"Inchworm" hand up ruler.

Continue cutting.

5. Every two or three strips, check to be certain your strips are perpendicular to the fold of the fabric. If not, follow step 3 to straighten the edge.

Casual Tip

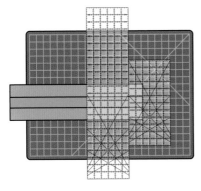

I also use the two-ruler method for cutting segments from strip sets. To cut with greatest accuracy, place a horizontal line on the cutting ruler along one of the central seam lines on the strip set. Don't worry if the top or bottom edge of the strip set is uneven. Focus on making accurate cuts perpendicular to the seam line.

Piecing

"It is better to be consistently inaccurate than inconsistently accurate."

The Casual Quilter

After many years of piecing quilts together, I've come to some conclusions. These tips may not be what you are accustomed to, because they follow the casual-quilting attitude that if you like it, it works.

- Some pieced quilts require perfect ¼" seams in order to get the points and seams to match. This is not true for the quilts in this book. Don't tell the Quilt Police, but it is more important to sew an even and consistent seam allowance when making these patterns than it is to hit the ¼" mark perfectly.

- My sewing machine tends to gulp thread at the beginning, only to regurgitate it like a hairball on the bottom piece of fabric. To avoid this in my patchwork, I start and stop on small scraps of fabric. I keep reusing these scraps until the cat steals them or the thread buildup makes it hard to feed them through the machine.

- When possible, I take an assembly-line approach to sewing, feeding pieces through the machine one after the other, stopping and cutting the thread only when an entire group is sewn. This is called chain piecing.

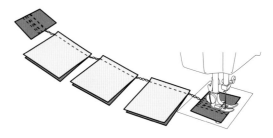

- I concentrate on getting opposing seams to match and let everything else fall where it may. If seam allowances are pressed in opposite directions, the seams match up more easily. When necessary, I pull, push, stretch, and ease the fabric to make the seams match. (Don't tell the Quilt Police!)

- I seldom pin pieces together before sewing. I make certain the seam allowances on seams that are supposed to match are pressed in opposite directions and then use my fingers to pinch and regulate the fabric as I feed it under the presser foot. About half my students like this technique, while the others get better results when they pin. If it works, you are doing it correctly. If you use pins, remove them just before you would cross over them with your needle.

- Sometimes, when one portion of the seam allowance has already been stitched down, such as when you are stitching rows together, you will find opposing seams pressed in the same direction, making them hard to sew accurately. There are several solutions. My favorite is to finger-press one seam in the opposite direction before sewing. The disadvantage to this is that it can cause a twist in the seam allowance, causing a tiny lump on the front of the quilt. The lump usually disappears, but if it bothers you, cut a ⅛" notch in the seam allowance where the twist occurs.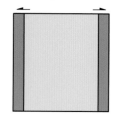

- I don't care if it is called pressing or ironing, the idea is to get the fabric to lie flat without stretching it out of shape. (I am a pro at turning my quilts into soft sculptures by stretching the fabric out of shape when I iron it.) Watch out for pleats along the seam lines as you iron. If I press pleats into a seam allowance, press a seam allowance in the wrong direction, or press a seam line out of shape, I spray a little water on it, fluff it, fold it back into the shape it had before pressing, and iron it flat. I then open the seam and iron again. I iron more accurately without steam, but most people prefer steam.

- Mistakes happen, and sometimes you just have to deal with them. It is frustrating to have to rip something out, substitute fabric, make the quilt smaller, or compromise the original design, but if there is no other way to make the quilt look like an achievement, that is what you have to do. I hate ripping out more than I dislike wasting fabric, so I often cut and sew more units or blocks than I need for the quilt. That way I can use the best and ignore the rest.

Adding Borders

"Let your quilt decide what borders it likes."
The Casual Quilter

I make my final decision on the number, size, and fabrics of borders after the center of the quilt top is completed. I take the top to the quilt shop and audition different fabrics against it. It is humbling how often my original choice changes.

You do not need to border your quilt if you do not want to. Borders do not have to be the same width, or made from the same fabrics. I have included widths and yardage for borders as a starting point only. If you use different measurements, remember to cut the border strips ½" wider than the desired finished width.

By the time a quilt's piecing is complete, there is a good chance that it lists a little because one side is longer than the side opposite. My quilts began to look a lot better when I learned how to use borders to square a lopsided quilt. Here's how:

1. Measure the length of the quilt top through the center. Cut two side border strips to this measurement. (If the border is longer than 42", you will need to sew two or three strips together, end to end, then trim to the correct length.) Mark the midpoints of the border strips and quilt top.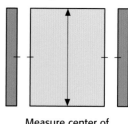

   Measure center of quilt, top to bottom.

2. With right sides together and raw edges, ends, and midpoints matching, sew the borders to the sides of the quilt top, easing as necessary. Press the seam allowances toward the border strips.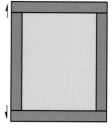

   Match ends and midpoints.

3. Measure the width of the quilt top through the center, including the side borders you just added. Cut two border strips to this measurement, piecing as necessary. Mark the midpoints of the border strips and quilt top. With right sides together and raw edges, ends, and midpoints matching, sew the top and bottom borders to the quilt top, easing as necessary. Press the seam allowances toward the border strips.

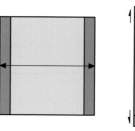

Match ends and midpoints.

Do Your Own Thing

Serenity by Robin Strobel, 2001, Issaquah, Washington, 52" x 68".

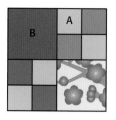
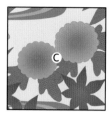

Pieced block
Finished size: 8" x 8"

C square
Finished size: 8" x 8"

Trish Carey is a friend who loves casual quilts. When she was a manager at In The Beginning Fabrics, she created a four-patch-variation quilt to inspire her customers to use a large decorator print (see "Trish's Do Your Own Thing," page 14). With her permission, I am including instructions for one of the many possibilities based on this simple design. You may decide to use many fabrics, or only a few; color-coordinate the four-patch units or let the colors fall randomly; or use several different fabrics for the B square. I hope this quilt starts your imagination wandering and you let yourself think "What if …" Take this design and "do your own thing."

Make It Easy

- This is a perfect quilt to show off a favorite fabric, large print, or directional pattern in the C squares. Choose the main fabric and work the others around it. Fat-quarter packets work well for the squares needed for the four-patch units. Don't be afraid to throw in a bright or contrasting color here and there. You can use any number of fabrics in the four-patch units.

Nondirectional prints   *Directional prints*

- There are two ways to make this quilt. The first, the traditional method, is to cut all of the squares the sizes indicated in the chart on page 11 and then assemble the top. I find this method works best if I am using a directional print for fabric 1 or fabric 2 (B and C squares). But if you are new to quilting, have trouble with an accurate or consistent ¼" seam, or just want to try something different, use the second method: cut only the 2½" x 2½" squares to begin, then follow the instructions under "Block Assembly" on page 12.

- Regardless of the method I use to piece the quilt, I like to make a stack of four-patch units and audition them against fabrics 1 and 2. Then I can decide to swap out one of the four-patch fabrics or throw in one or two new squares from my stash. In making "Serenity," I originally planned to use a wide range of blue (and only blue) fabrics for the four-patch units. My intention was to follow the rule that a proper design has a full range of value. But after I created a stack of four-patch units, I found that I did not like the harshness of dark blue against the romantic, large floral pattern I'd chosen for the C squares. I kept making four-patch units from different fabrics until I found I liked the muted look of some orange prints, a few medium blues that provided a touch of contrast, and a green that appears nowhere in the featured fabric. Don't tell the Quilt Police, but I ended up liking a design containing fabrics in a narrow range of values and with an overabundance of gold and orange. In addition, I decided to make the quilt larger than I had planned, and ran out of fabric 2. No problem, I just added another gold print. If I'd kept quiet about all of this, would you know that my original color plan was not very attractive, and that I ran out of fabric and had to substitute? Or would you think that I brilliantly preplanned everything in detail? A Casual Quilter knows when to keep her mouth shut!

Quilt Information

	Lap	Twin	Double	Queen	King
Finished size with borders	52" x 68"	68" x 84"	84" x 92"	92" x 100"	108" x 108"
Blocks wide x blocks tall	5 x 7	7 x 9	9 x 10	10 x 11	12 x 12
No. of pieced blocks	18	32	45	55	72
No. of C squares	17	31	45	55	72

Materials • 42"-wide fabric

	Lap	Twin	Double	Queen	King
Fabric 1 for B and C squares	1¾ yds.	2⅝ yds.	3⅞ yds.	4⅝ yds.	5⅞ yds.
Fabric 2 for B squares	½ yd.	⅝ yd.	⅞ yd.	1⅛ yds.	1¼ yds.
Fabrics 3–12 for A squares	¼ yd. *each*	¼ yd. *each*	⅜ yd. *each*	⅜ yd. *each*	⅜ yd. *each*
Inner border	⅜ yd.	½ yd.	½ yd.	½ yd.	⅝ yd.
Outer border	1⅛ yd.	1¼ yds.	1⅝ yds.	1⅝ yds.	1⅞ yds.
Backing	3¾ yds.	5¾ yds.	8⅝ yds.	9 yds.	10½ yds.
Binding	½ yd.	⅝ yd.	¾ yd.	¾ yd.	⅞ yd.
Batting	Twin size	Twin size	Queen size	King size	King size

Cutting

	Lap	Twin	Double	Queen	King
From fabric 1, cut:*					
8½" x 42" strips	5	8	12	14	18
Crosscut into C squares, each 8½" x 8½"	17	31	45	55	72
4½" x 42" strips	2	4	5	7	8
Crosscut into B squares, each 4½" x 4½"	18	32	45	55	72
From fabric 2, cut:*					
4½" x 42" strips	2	4	5	7	8
Crosscut into B squares, each 4½" x 4½"	18	32	45	55	72
From fabrics 3–12, cut:**					
2½" x 42" strips from *each*	1	2	3	3	4
Crosscut into A squares, each 2½" x 2½"	144 *total*	256 *total*	360 *total*	440 *total*	576 *total*
From fabric for inner border, cut:					
1½" x 42" strips	5	7	8	8	10
From fabric for outer border, cut:					
5½" x 42" strips	6	7	9	9	11
From fabric for binding, cut:					
2¼" x 42" strips	6	8	9	10	11

*You may cut the squares as indicated, or cut as indicated in step 4 on page 12 and step 7 on page 13.

**The number of strips will vary if you use a different number of fabrics to make the four-patch units, or use the fabrics in different proportions. Remember that you are working on your quilt—not mine. You can change the rules as you go along.*

Block Assembly

1. Refer to "Make It Easy" on page 10 to select fabrics 1–12.

2. To make the four-patch units, with right sides together, stitch the 2½" x 2½" A squares into pairs. Chain-piecing (see page 7) makes this very quick. Press the seam allowances toward the darker fabric. Sew 2 pairs together as shown to complete a four-patch unit. Press the seam allowance in either direction. You may consistently pair the same fabrics (like Trish did in "Trish's Do Your Own Thing" on page 14), or pair the fabrics randomly (like I did in "Summer Beaches" on page 14). Traditionally, four-patch units are made up of 2 lighter fabric squares that oppose each other diagonally and 2 darker fabric squares that oppose each other diagonally.

Four-patch unit

3. Measure your four-patch units. If your cutting and sewing are perfect, they will measure 4½" x 4½". Don't worry; perfect cutting and sewing are not required for this pattern. Ask yourself the following questions: Are the four-patch units close to the same size? Are they (mostly) square? If the sizes vary widely (¼" or more), take the time to trim the four-patch units down to the smallest size—whatever that measurement is. When trimming, try to keep the intersection of the 4 squares centered. Some people love to trim all their four-patch units so they match perfectly. Personally, I hate trimming and only do it if my four-patch units are extremely irregular.

Trim, centering
intersection of squares.

Casual Tip

Make more four-patch units than you need. Use only the "best" ones on the front, and sew the others together for part of the quilt back, save them for another project, or (gasp!) just toss them.

4. Cut the number of B squares indicated in the cutting chart, but instead of cutting them 4½" x 4½", cut fabric 1 and fabric 2 into squares the same dimensions as your four-patch units. (Remember, 4½" is just the measurement of a "perfectly" sewn four-patch unit.) For example, if you are making a twin-size quilt and your four-patch units measure 4⅛" x 4⅛", cut fabric 1 into 4 strips, each 4⅛" x 42", and crosscut the strips into 32 squares, each 4⅛" x 4⅛".

5. To make each pieced block, sew 2 four-patch units, 1 B square in fabric 1, and 1 B square in fabric 2 together as shown. I find it easiest to sew with the four-patch unit on top. Be careful to stitch the correct edges together. Press the seam allowances in the direction indicated.

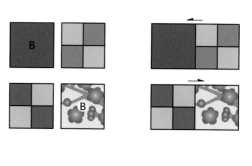

Pieced block

6. Measure the pieced blocks. Are they the same size? Are they square? Sound familiar? If the sizes vary widely (⅜" or more—larger blocks give a little more easing room), take the time to trim the larger pieced blocks down to the size of the smallest. Remember, when trimming, to try to keep the intersection of the 4 large pieces centered.

7. Cut the number of C squares indicated in the cutting chart from fabric 1, but instead of cutting them 8½" x 8½", cut them the same dimensions as your pieced blocks. (Remember, 8½" is just the measurement of a "perfectly" sewn block.) For example, if you are making a twin-size quilt and your pieced blocks measure 8⅛" x 8⅛", you will cut fabric 1 into 8 strips, 8⅛" x 42", and crosscut the strips into 31 squares, each 8⅛" x 8⅛".

Quilt-Top Assembly

1. Refer to the quilt assembly diagram to arrange the pieced blocks and C squares into horizontal rows. Sew the blocks in each row together. Press the seam allowances toward the C squares. Sew the rows together. Press the seam allowances in one direction.

2. Refer to "Adding Borders" on page 8 to cut border strips to size and to stitch the inner border and then the outer border to the quilt top. Notice that "Summer Beaches" on page 14 does not have borders.

Quilt Finishing

1. Layer the backing, batting, and quilt top; baste the layers together.
2. Quilt as desired.
3. Bind the quilt edges.

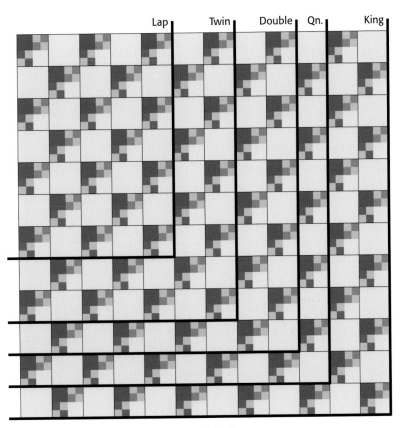

Quilt Assembly Diagram

Casual Tip

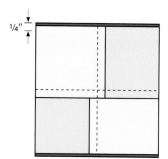 When the four-patch unit does not measure the same size as the cut B square, first see how big the difference is. If the difference is less than ⅛", just split the difference and sew the pieces together, using a ¼" seam.

If the difference is more than ⅛", I determine which is inaccurate, the four-patch unit or the B square. I put the inaccurate piece aside. Because I usually make more pieces than are needed I may not have to bother with figuring out what is wrong. But if it turns out I need more pieces in the quilt top, I look through my rejects. If for some reason the piece is too large, I cut it down to the correct size. If it is too small, I use it only if I absolutely have to. It will have to be fussed and maybe resewn, and the fabrics around it stretched and eased. This usually makes the top look a little lumpy. Fortunately, pressing and quilting can take care of most of these evils.

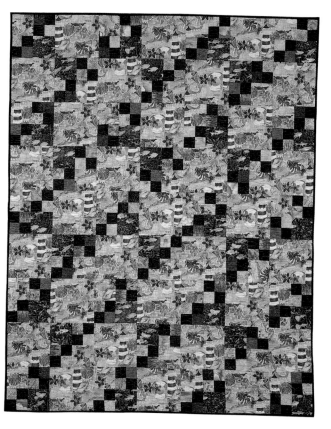

Summer Beaches by Robin Strobel, 2001, Issaquah, Washington, 58" x 73½". Quilted by Janice Nelson.

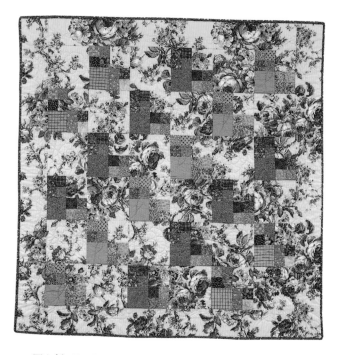

Trish's Do Your Own Thing by Trish Carey, 1994, Issaquah, Washington, 54" x 54".

Domino

· ·

Domino by Robin Strobel, 1998, Issaquah, Washington, 44" x 62". Quilted by Janice Nelson.

Domino
Finished size: 9" x 9"

Domino is a traditional pattern that dates back to the Depression. At that time quilting was extremely popular in the United States, and many newspapers carried daily or weekly columns containing quilt patterns. According to Barbara Brackman's *Encyclopedia of Pieced Quilt Patterns*, Domino Net first appeared in Nancy Cabot's column in the *Chicago Tribune* in 1937.

I love the simplicity and versatility of a Domino quilt. It requires only four different fabrics, yet the blocks can be rotated to create many variations. Best of all, the pattern works with a wide range of fabrics. Go for bold and bright, soft and floral, or country and folk fabrics.

Make It Easy

- Don't worry too much about your fabric selections. This is one of the few patterns where I let different values fall where they may. You can place light or dark fabric in any of the positions. If you like the way the four fabrics look together, the pattern will work.

- I often choose different colors or values for fabrics 2 and 3 to divide the block visually along the diagonal. It is difficult to know which way each block will be rotated in the quilt, so I avoid fabrics with a very strong directional print, such as cows standing in a field. (With my luck, I'd end up sewing one block with tipped-over cows.)

*Upside-down
directional print*

- Pay attention to cutting accurate strip widths.
- When sewing the strip sets together, try to sew consistent seam allowances. I don't worry too much about having a perfect ¼" seam. Consistency is more important than accuracy.
- Domino quilts tend to develop their own personality. I advise you to finish all the blocks, then play with the arrangement. Often the arrangement you end up liking is not the one you had in mind when you started. When I told one of my beginning students this, she replied, "If it starts developing its own personality, this quilt can darn well sew itself together!" Inevitably, the block arrangement she liked best was not the one she started with. I am happy to say that though the quilt adamantly refused to sew itself together, it was completed and loved.

Quilt Information

	Wall/baby	Long lap	Square lap	Twin	Double	Queen	King
Finished size with borders	44" x 44"	44" x 62"	62" x 62"	66" x 84"	75" x 84"	84" x 102"	102" x 102"
Blocks wide x blocks tall	4 x 4	4 x 6	6 x 6	6 x 8	7 x 8	8 x 10	10 x 10
No. of pieced blocks	16	24	36	48	56	80	100

Materials • 42"-wide fabric

	Wall/baby	Long lap	Square lap	Twin	Double	Queen	King
Fabric 1	¾ yd.	1 yd.	1 ¼ yds.	1 ⅝ yds.	1 ⅞ yds.	2 ½ yds.	3 ⅛ yds.
Fabric 2	⅝ yd.	⅞ yd.	1 yd.	1 ⅜ yds.	1 ⅝ yds.	2 ⅛ yds.	2 ½ yds.
Fabric 3	⅝ yd.	⅞ yd.	1 yd.	1 ⅜ yds.	1 ⅝ yds.	2 ⅛ yds.	2 ½ yds.
Fabric 4	½ yd.	¾ yd.	⅞ yd.	1 ⅛ yds.	1 ⅛ yds.	1 ½ yds.	2 yds.
Inner border	¼ yd.	⅜ yd.	⅜ yd.	½ yd.	½ yd.	⅝ yd.	¾ yd.
Outer border	⅝ yd.	⅝ yd.	¾ yd.	1 ¼ yds.	1 ¼ yds.	1 ⅜ yds.	1 ½ yds.
Backing	3 ¼ yds.	3 ¼ yds.	4 ¼ yds.	5 ¾ yds.	5 ¾ yds.	8 ⅝ yds.	10 ¼ yds.
Binding	½ yd.	½ yd.	½ yd.	⅝ yd.	⅝ yd.	¾ yd.	¾ yd.
Batting	Crib size	Twin size	Twin size	Twin size	Double size	Queen size	King size

Cutting

	Wall/baby	Long lap	Square lap	Twin	Double	Queen	King
From fabric 1, cut:							
2" x 42" strips	4	8	8	12	12	16	20
3½" x 42" strips	3	4	6	8	10	14	17
From fabric 2, cut:							
2" x 42" strips	6	9	12	16	19	26	32
3½" x 42" strips	1	2	2	3	3	4	5
From fabric 3, cut:							
2" x 42" strips	6	9	12	16	19	26	32
3½" x 42" strips	1	2	2	3	3	4	5
From fabric 4, cut:							
2" x 42" strips	6	10	12	16	18	24	30
From fabric for inner border, cut:							
1½" x 42" strips	4	5	6	–	–	–	–
2" x 42" strips	–	–	–	6	7	9	10
From fabric for outer border, cut:							
3½" x 42" strips	4	5	6	–	–	–	–
5" x 42" strips	–	–	–	8	8	9	10
From fabric for binding, cut:							
2¼" x 42" strips	5	6	6	8	8	9	10

Casual Tip

 Fabrics 2 and 3 are cut into identical strips. You can reduce the number of cuts you have to make by half if you layer the two fabrics together (see page 6).

Block Assembly

1. With right sides together and raw edges aligned, sew a 2" x 42" fabric 2 strip to a 2" x 42" fabric 4 strip along the long edges to make strip set A. Remember, keeping consistent seam allowances will help when assembling the quilt later. Press the seam allowance toward the fabric 4 strip.

Make the number of strip sets indicated in the strip set A chart on page 19.

Strip Set A

2. Layer two A strip sets right sides together so the fabrics alternate as shown. Crosscut the paired strip sets into the number of 2"-wide segments indicated in the strip set A chart on page 19. If you have an uneven number of strip sets, cut 1 in half widthwise and layer the 2 halves. Once the pieces are cut, keep them sandwiched together—they are ready for the sewing machine!

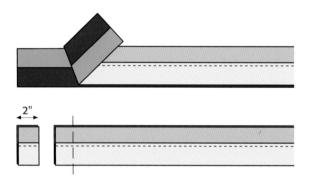

2"

Casual Tip

The minimum number of cut segments needed is indicated in each chart. I always cut as many segments as fabric allows because it is easier to throw away extra or inaccurate crosscuts than it is to go back and cut more.

3. Sew the paired 2" segments from step 2 into four-patch units as shown. It is a good idea to orient all of the pieces the same way as you feed them through the sewing machine. Try to keep the paired segment oriented so that fabric 4 is at the top, as shown; this is not essential, but it will make the sewing in step 9 easier. Press the

seams in either direction. Refer to "Quilt Information" on page 16 for the number of blocks in your quilt; you will need 1 four-patch unit from strip set A for each block.

4. Repeat steps 1–3 with the 2" x 42" fabric 3 and fabric 4 strips to make strip set B. Refer to the strip set B chart on page 19 for the number of strip sets to make and 2"-wide segments to crosscut. Sew the four-patch units together with fabric 4 at the top. Press the seams in either direction. You will need 1 four-patch unit from strip set B for each block in your quilt.

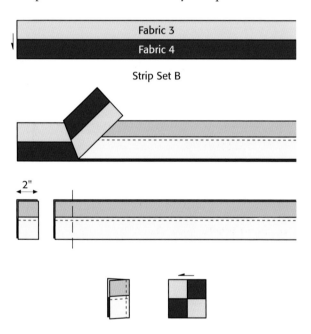

Strip Set B

2"

5. Sew the remaining 2" x 42" and 3½" x 42" strips together as shown on page 19 to make strip sets C, D, and E. Refer to the charts on page 19 to crosscut the strips into segments. (Note that strip set E should be crosscut into 3½"-wide segments—I have been known to get carried away and crosscut it into 2"-wide segments. The only way to salvage that situation is to buy more fabric and re-create the strip set.) For each block in your quilt, you will need 1 segment from each of strip sets C and D, and 2 segments from strip set E.

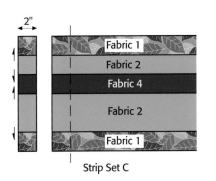
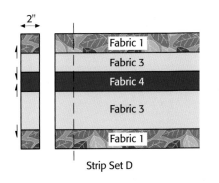
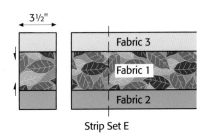

Strip Set C

Strip Set D

Strip Set E

Strip Set A

	Wall/baby	Long lap	Square lap	Twin	Double	Queen	King
No. of strip sets	2	3	4	5	6	8	10
No. of 2" segments to crosscut	32	48	72	96	112	160	200

Strip Set B

	Wall/baby	Long lap	Square lap	Twin	Double	Queen	King
No. of strip sets	2	3	4	5	6	8	10
No. of 2" segments to crosscut	32	48	72	96	112	160	200

Strip Set C

	Wall/baby	Long lap	Square lap	Twin	Double	Queen	King
No. of strip sets	1	2	2	3	3	4	5
No. of 2" segments to crosscut	16	24	36	48	56	80	100

Strip Set D

	Wall/baby	Long lap	Square lap	Twin	Double	Queen	King
No. of strip sets	1	2	2	3	3	4	5
No. of 2" segments to crosscut	16	24	36	48	56	80	100

Strip Set E

	Wall/baby	Long lap	Square lap	Twin	Double	Queen	King
No. of strip sets	3	4	6	8	10	14	17
No. of 3½" segments to crosscut	32	48	72	96	112	160	200

6. For each block, arrange the strip set C, D, and E segments and four-patch units as shown, being careful to orient them correctly. Fabric 4, the accent fabric, creates a 3-square chain across 2 of the corners. The large and small squares of fabric 1 will divide the block along the diagonal with fabric 2 on one side and fabric 3 on the other.

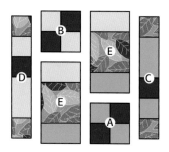

7. Sew the strip set A and strip set B four-patch units to the strip set E segments. Be certain the four-patch units are positioned correctly. Press the seam allowances toward the four-patch units.

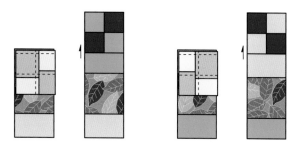

8. Lay out the block again. Check the orientation of the units. Stitch the vertical rows together. Press the seam allowances in one direction.

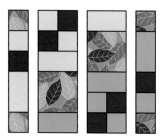 

Casual Tip

After I make one block, I like to keep it where I can refer to it as I sew the other blocks together.

Quilt-Top Assembly

1. When you have completed the blocks, it is time to play with their layout, or "set." Experiment with different arrangements until you find one you like; then step back, run some errands, and get some coffee before coming back and playing with the arrangement some more. If you have a digital or Polaroid camera, it helps to take quick shots of the different arrangements you like. Here are just a few of the possibilities.

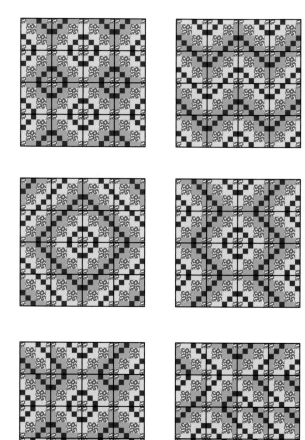

2. Refer to the quilt assembly diagram to arrange the blocks into horizontal rows. Sew the blocks in each row together. Press the seam allowances in opposite directions from row to row. Sew the rows together. Press the seam allowances in one direction.

3. Refer to "Adding Borders" on page 8 to cut the border strips to size and to stitch the inner border and then the outer border to the quilt top.

Quilt Finishing

1. Layer the backing, batting, and quilt top; baste the layers together.
2. Quilt as desired.
3. Bind the quilt edges.

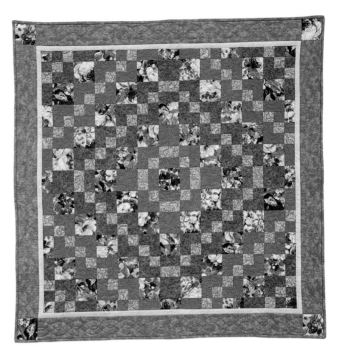

Domino Trip by Robin Strobel, 1999, Issaquah, Washington, 44" x 44".

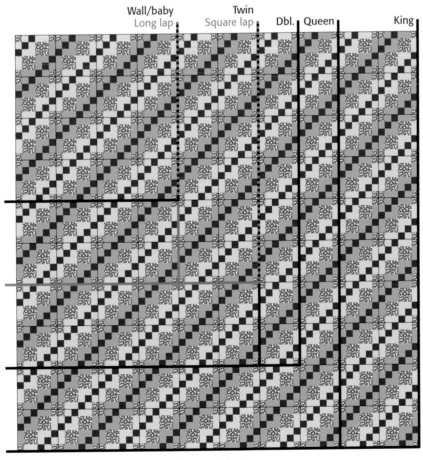

Quilt Assembly Diagram

Basic Tipsy Nine Patch

Fishes by Robin Strobel, 1999, Issaquah, Washington, 40" x 58". Quilted by Janice Nelson.

Basic Tipsy Nine Patch
Finished sizes:
6" x 6" or 8" x 8"

This pattern gives new meaning to "stacking and whacking." Unlike the popular pattern to which that phrase refers, this technique requires no careful layering, fussy-cutting, or examination of pattern repeats. In the last six years, I have experimented with several variations on this technique. Sometimes I slash the squares in curved lines in the manner of Nancy Crow. Sometimes when I set the blocks, I alternate the tipsy blocks with plain squares of fabric. If you plan ahead, you can make stars, trees, and other shapes. Play with it and have fun.

I am presenting two variations of this pattern. In this version, the Basic Tipsy Nine Patch, you create the blocks and simply sew them together to make the quilt top. In the second variation, Truly Tipsy Nine Patch (page 28), you create the blocks and sew background triangles onto them to make the blocks "tip." This creates a beautiful quilt, but I must warn you, it takes twice as long as the basic version.

Make It Easy

- This pattern works best if you choose at least nine fabrics that are visually distinct from one another. By this I mean that when you place the fabrics next to each other, the edges are apparent; the fabrics do not blur together. If you use more than nine fabrics, you must increase in multiples of three (twelve, fifteen, eighteen) because you need nine different fabrics to make each block.

Depending on the size of quilt you make, this may result in one or two leftover blocks. Just save the leftovers for another project or incorporate them into the backing.

Individual fabrics stand out.

Fabrics blend together too much.

- Sewing Tipsy Nine Patch blocks is fast. Your pieces do not have to be cut exactly to the correct measurement. They do not have to be stacked perfectly. Your seams do not need to be accurate or even. If the edges of the sewn blocks are too ragged, you will trim them. There is only one little thing you have to be careful about …

  After you slash the squares and sew the segments together, be very, very careful you do not turn or flip the individual pieces. I take a very systematic approach to sewing these blocks, slashing, arranging, and stitching one group before going on to the next.

- For every square you start with, you will get one Nine Patch block. The finished Nine Patch block will be about 1½" smaller than your original square. For example, if you cut 7½" squares to start, your finished blocks will measure about 6". If you start with 9½" squares, your finished blocks will measure about 8".

- Lap, twin, and double quilts start with 7½" squares; queen- and king-size quilts start with 9½" squares.

Quilt Information

	Lap	Twin	Double	Queen	King
Finished size with borders	40" x 58"	64" x 82"	82" x 94"	90" x 98"	106" x 106"
Blocks wide x blocks tall	5 x 8	9 x 12	12 x 14	10 x 11	12 x 12
No. of pieced blocks	40	108	168	110	144

Materials • 42"-wide fabric

	Lap	Twin	Double	Queen	King
9 to 18 assorted fabrics	2¼ yds. *total*	5⅛ yds. *total*	7¾ yds. *total*	8¼ yds. *total*	10⅜ yds. *total*
Inner border	¼ yd.	⅜ yd.	⅜ yd.	⅜ yd.	⅜ yd.
Outer border	⅞ yd.	1⅛ yds.	1½ yds.	1½ yds.	1¾ yds.
Backing	3 yds.	5¼ yds.	8⅝ yds.	9 yds.	10½ yds.
Binding	½ yd.	⅝ yd.	¾ yd.	¾ yd.	⅞ yd.
Batting	Twin size	Twin size	Queen size	King size	King size

Cutting

	Lap	Twin	Double	Queen	King
From 9 to 18 assorted fabrics, cut:					
7½" x 7½" squares	42 *total**	108 *total**	168 *total**	–	–
9½" x 9½" squares	–	–	–	111 *total**	144 *total**
From fabric for inner border, cut:					
1" x 42" strips	4	7	8	9	10
From fabric for outer border, cut:					
5" x 42" strips	5	7	9	9	11
From fabric for binding, cut:					
2¼" x 42" strips	5	7	9	9	11

This is the minimum number of squares needed to make the Nine Patch blocks. If you want to cut an equal number of squares from each fabric, divide the total given by the number of fabrics being used, then round up to the nearest whole number. For example, if you are using 9 fabrics and making the lap-size quilt, you would divide 42 by 9 for a total of 4.66. You would need to cut 5 squares from each of the 9 fabrics for a total of 45 squares.

Block Assembly

1. Put the squares of each fabric into a separate pile. Divide the piles into groups, with 3 different fabrics in each group. You will have 3 to 6 groups, depending on the number of different fabrics you are using in the quilt. Number the fabrics in each group 1–3.

2. Pick any one of the groups to begin. Stack a square of fabric 1, a square of fabric 2, and a square of fabric 3, right sides facing up.

3. With a rotary cutter and ruler, slice vertically across the stack twice, dividing the squares into 3 segments. I use a ruler to get a straight cut and to stabilize the fabric. Make the cuts at different angles, and make sure the pieces are no narrower than 1" at any point.

1" or wider

4. Separate the segments on the left-hand side of the cut squares and place them in 3 vertical rows as shown. Be certain the orientation of each segment remains the same. Do not rotate or flip the pieces!

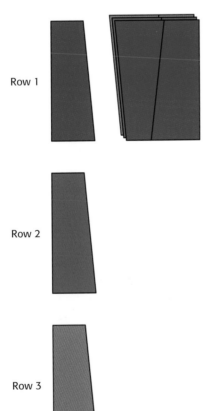

Row 1

Row 2

Row 3

5. Separate the segments in the center of the cut squares in the same manner, laying the pieces beside the segments from the left-hand side of the squares. Repeat for the segments on the right-hand side of the cut squares, laying the pieces beside the segments from the center. Arrange the pieces so the same fabric does not appear more than once in any row.

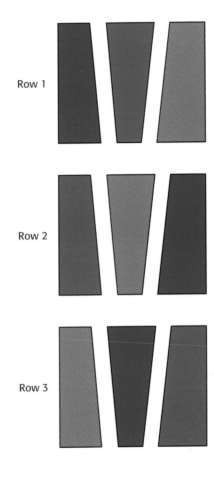

Row 1

Row 2

Row 3

6. Using a ¼" seam allowance, stitch the segments in each horizontal row together. Be very careful to sew the correct edges together and keep the fabrics oriented in the same direction as when they were cut. I always sew column A to column B and then add column C in an extremely systematic fashion so I am less likely to mix things up. Press the seam allowances in one direction.

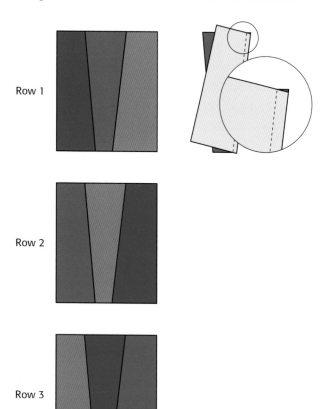

Row 1

Row 2

Row 3

7. Repeat steps 2–6 with the remaining squares in the group, then with the squares in each of the remaining groups. Vary the angle at which you cut each group of 3 squares. Experiment with parallel slashes, and wider and narrower cuts. Keep the pieced squares from each group in separate piles.

8. Select 3 pieced squares, each from a different group, and stack them on top of each other, right sides facing up and with the seams running horizontally.

9. Slice the stack twice vertically, altering the angle of the slices as in step 3.

10. Referring to steps 4 and 5, separate the segments into 3 vertical rows.

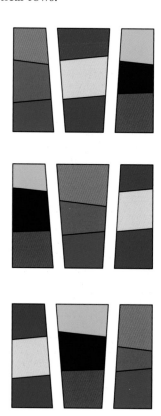

11. Stitch the segments in each horizontal row together. Press the seam allowances in one direction.

12. Repeat steps 8–11 with the remaining pieced units. After constructing all of the Nine Patch blocks, check the size of each one. Square up the blocks by trimming any excess. If some blocks are larger than the others, trim to the smallest size.

Quilt-Top Assembly

1. Refer to the quilt assembly diagram to arrange the blocks into horizontal rows. Try not to obsess too much over placement. Sew the blocks in each row together. Press the seam allowances in opposite directions from row to row. Sew the rows together. Press the seam allowances in one direction.

2. Refer to "Adding Borders" on page 8 to cut the border strips to size and to stitch the inner and then the outer borders to the quilt top.

Quilt Finishing

1. Layer the backing, batting, and quilt top; baste the layers together.
2. Quilt as desired.
3. Bind the quilt edges.

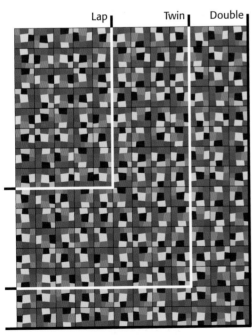

Quilt Assembly Diagram
(6" blocks)

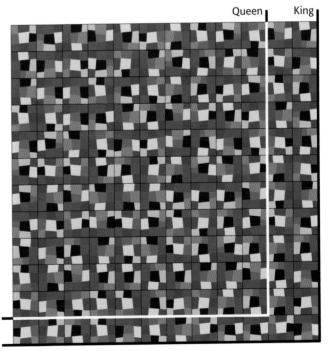

Quilt Assembly Diagram
(8" blocks)

Truly Tipsy Nine Patch

Dad's Quilt by Robin Strobel, 1999, Issaquah, Washington, 54½" x 77". Quilted by Janice Nelson.

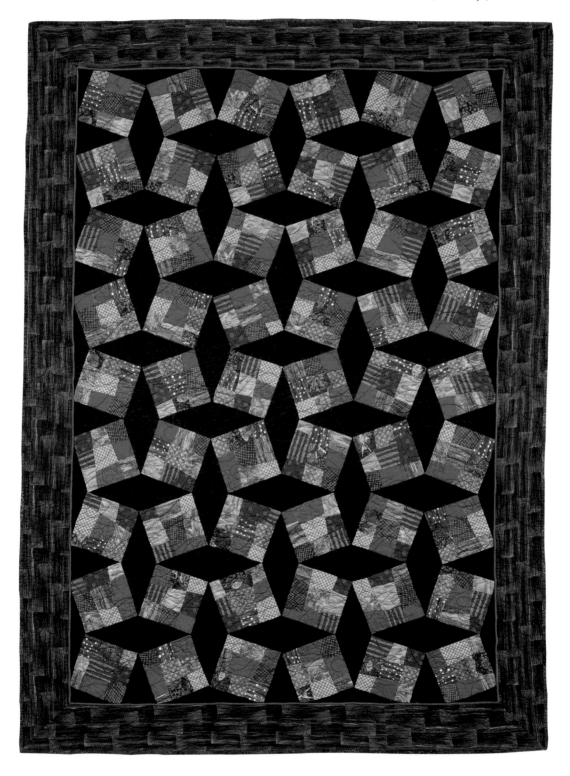

Truly Tipsy Nine Patch
Finished size: 7½" x 7½"

Add a wonderful visual twist to the Basic Tipsy Nine Patch block by stitching background triangles to each side of the block. If you want a dramatic-looking quilt, choose a fabric for the triangles that will set off the nine-patch units, as I did here. Choosing a medium-sized floral print for the triangles, as in "Tipsy Plaids" (page 32), creates an entirely different, softer look. Both of these quilts use twelve fabrics for the nine-patch units. I have based my instructions on that number, but you can use anywhere from nine to ninety different fabrics. You will end up with one nine-patch unit for every plain square you cut.

Let your border fabrics decide the width they should be cut. The only reason I chose to make a very narrow inner border for "Dad's Quilt" (page 28) was to keep the strong red from overpowering the blocks. I usually avoid ¼" borders because they are hard to sew evenly. I auditioned ½" inner borders from the red, but then my eyes just wanted to focus on the border, not the quilt. "Tipsy Plaids" has a reasonable ¾" finished inner border.

Quilt Information

	Small lap	Lap	Twin	Double
Finished size with borders	47" x 62"	54½" x 77"	69½" x 92"	84½" x 92"
Blocks wide x blocks tall	5 x 7	6 x 9	8 x 11	10 x 11
No. of pieced blocks	35	54	88	110

Materials • *42"-wide fabric*

	Small lap	Lap	Twin	Double
12 assorted fabrics for nine-patch units	⅜ yd. *each*	⅜ yd. *each*	⅝ yd. *each*	⅝ yd. *each*
Coordinating fabric for background triangles	1½ yds.	2 yds.	3 yds.	3¾ yds.
Inner border	¼ yd.	¼ yd.	¼ yd.	¼ yd.
Outer border	⅞ yd.	1 yd.	1⅛ yds.	1⅜ yds.
Backing	3 yds.	3¼ yds.	5¾ yds.	5¾ yds.
Binding	½ yd.	⅝ yd.	⅝ yd.	¾ yd.
Batting	Crib size	Twin size	Twin size	Double size

Cutting

	Small lap	Lap	Twin	Double
From 12 assorted fabrics, cut:				
7½" x 7½" squares	36 *total**	54 *total**	90 *total**	111 *total**
From coordinating fabric, cut:				
8⅝" x 42" strips	5	7	11	14
Crosscut into 2½" x 8⅝" rectangles	70	108	176	220
From fabric for inner border, cut:				
¾" x 42" strips	5	6	7	8
From fabric for outer border, cut:				
5" x 42" strips	5	6	7	8
From fabric for binding, cut:				
2¼" x 42" strips	6	7	8	9

This is the minimum number of squares needed to make the Nine Patch blocks. If you want to cut an equal number of squares from each fabric, divide the total given by the number of fabrics being used, then round up to the nearest whole number. For example, if you are using 12 fabrics and making the lap-size quilt, you would divide 54 by 12 for a total of 4.5. You would need to cut 5 squares from each of the 12 fabrics for a total of 60 squares.

Block Assembly

1. Referring to the instructions for Basic Tipsy Nine Patch on pages 22–27 and "Quilt Information" on page 29, make 1 nine-patch unit for each block of your quilt.

2. Place two 2½" x 8⅝" rectangles right sides together. Cut the pair of rectangles in half diagonally. This effectively cuts one rectangle from the upper right corner to the lower left corner and the other rectangle from the upper left corner to the lower right corner. Repeat for the remaining rectangles.

   Note: Because the small lap-size quilt is made up of an odd number of blocks, cut 17 pairs of rectangles in one direction and 18 pairs of rectangles in the opposite direction.

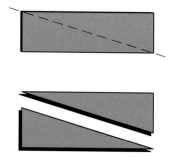

3. Separate the triangle on the top of each pair from the triangle on the bottom of each pair. When each set of triangles is turned right side up, half will reflect a left-to-right cut, and the other half will reflect a right-to-left cut. Put all of the right-to-left-cut triangles in one stack and all of the left-to-right-cut triangles in another stack. You will use one group of triangles with half of the nine-patch units and the other group with the remaining nine-patch units. This is what makes some blocks tip to the left and some tip to the right.

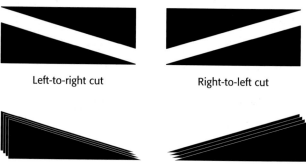

Left-to-right cut   Right-to-left cut

Make two stacks of triangles, all right side up.

4. Take a background triangle from one of the stacks from step 3. With right sides together, place the long, bias edge of the triangle against the top edge of a nine-patch unit, extending the wide end of the triangle slightly beyond the edge of the square. Working from the widest to the narrowest end of the triangle, stitch the background triangle to the nine-patch unit. Press the seam allowance toward the triangle.

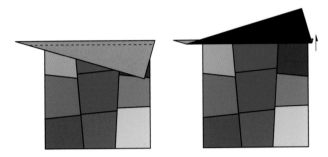

5. Using the same stack of triangles as you used in step 4, work around the nine-patch unit, stitching a background triangle to each of the remaining sides. Press the seam allowances toward the triangle after each addition. For half of the blocks, stitch the right-to-left-cut triangles to the nine-patch unit in a clockwise direction; for the remaining nine-patch units, stitch the left-to-right-cut triangles to the unit in a counterclockwise direction. (Be careful to sew the long, bias edge of each triangle to the nine-patch unit, not the straight-grain edge!) Trim the long "ears" at the tips of the triangles after the blocks are sewn.

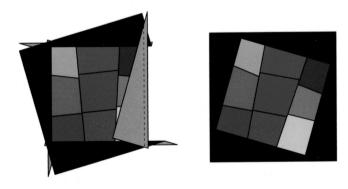

6. Repeat steps 4 and 5 with the remaining nine-patch units and background triangles. Half of the blocks should tip to the left and half should tip to the right.

Left-to-right-cut triangles

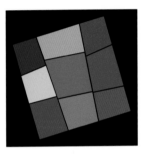

Right-to-left-cut triangles

7. If you want a tidy-looking quilt, trim any uneven blocks so there is ¼" for a seam allowance between the corners of the nine-patch unit and the outer edges of the background triangles. (I usually don't bother.)

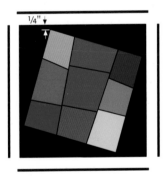

¼"

Quilt-Top Assembly

1. Refer to the quilt assembly diagram to arrange the blocks into horizontal rows, alternating right-tipped and left-tipped blocks. Sew the blocks in each row together. Sew the rows together. Press the seam allowances open to reduce bulk (the Quilt Police are going to arrest me some day for doing this).
2. Refer to "Adding Borders" on page 8 to cut the border strips to size and to stitch the inner and then the outer borders to the quilt top.

Quilt Finishing

1. Layer the backing, batting, and quilt top; baste the layers together.
2. Quilt as desired.
3. Bind the quilt edges.

Tipsy Plaids by Robin Strobel, 1998, Issaquah, Washington, 48" x 62". Quilted by Janice Nelson.

Quilt Assembly Diagram

Two Blocks Are Better Than One

Crabby Witches by Robin Strobel, 2000, Issaquah, Washington, 53" x 69".

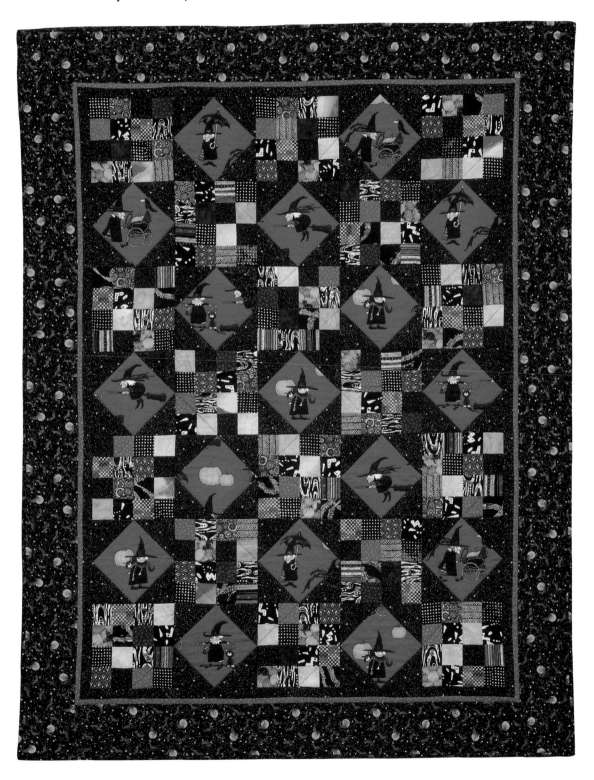

Block A
Sixteen Patch
Finished size: 8" x 8"

Block B
Square in a Square
Finished size: 8" x 8"

I was hanging out at QuiltWorks Northwest, my local quilt shop, when David Warner, the owner's husband, asked if I had noticed a wonderful Halloween fabric that they just received. David is more interested in computers and crunching numbers than in fabric, so a print that caught his attention had to be special. So began the "Crabby Witches" quilt. I knew the witches would lose their magic if they were chopped into little pieces, so I decided to fussy cut them for the center of a Square in a Square block. I chose a Sixteen Patch for the alternate block to show off the witches without competing with them. The Sixteen Patch blocks are made from black-and-white prints that alternate with bright prints to get a scrappy look. I know the witch fabric is pretty special, and will not be available when this book comes out (QuiltWorks sold out in two days!), but the pattern works with any print you fall in love with and want to feature.

Make It Easy

- When I want to fussy cut a print and the pattern I'm using doesn't call for fussy cutting, I buy two to three times the amount of fabric indicated in the pattern. I can't give hard and fast rules about fabric amounts because it depends on how large or small the pattern repeat is. I've given my best guess in the chart on page 35. Remember, if you buy more fabric than you need, you can always use the extra on the back of your quilt. If you run out of the fabric you want to feature, add a few squares of something that complements the featured print. This is a classic example of a mistake becoming an opportunity for creativity. Don't tell anyone you planned the quilt differently, and you will be known as a creative genius.

- If you decide not to use a large directional print for the center of block B, try a pretty floral or a fabric with a medium-to-large repeating design. Then there is no need to fussy cut; just hack out the squares and let the print fall where it may.

- Make the quilt even easier by cutting an 8½" x 8½" square of the block B focus fabric instead of making a Square in a Square block.

- There are several methods for making block B. The instructions here are for the method I feel is the most accurate and easiest to piece, although it wastes more fabric. The main advantage of this technique over the fabric-frugal method is that there are no raw bias edges to sew together and so the block does not stretch out of shape as easily. If you are fussy cutting to feature a design on the fabric, remember that the corner triangles will cover a portion of the square.

- For block A, I cut strips 2½" x 21" (selvage to center fold) when I want to mix many different fabrics together. If you are using only one fabric for the dark squares, like in "Dragon's Dance" (page 37), cut the strips 2½" x 42" (selvage to selvage), and cut only half the number of strips indicated of both the dark and light groups. Sew half the number of strip sets indicated, but cut the same number of segments from them.

Quilt Information

	Wall/baby	Lap	Twin	Double	Queen
Finished size with borders	35" x 35"	53" x 69"	71" x 87"	90" x 106"	110" x 110"
Blocks wide x blocks tall	3 x 3	5 x 7	7 x 9	9 x 11	11 x 11
No. of pieced A blocks	5	18	32	50	61
No. of pieced B blocks	4	17	31	49	60

Materials • *42"-wide fabric*

	Wall/baby	Lap	Twin	Double	Queen
6 black-and-white or dark prints for A blocks	⅛ yd. *each*	¼ yd. *each*	⅜ yd. *each*	½ yd. *each*	⅝ yd. *each*
12 bright or light prints for A blocks (6 for wall/baby size)	⅛ yd. *each*	¼ yd. *each*	¼ yd. *each*	⅜ yd. *each*	⅜ yd. *each*
Print for B block centers					
Straight cut	⅜ yd.	1⅜ yds.	2⅛ yds.	3⅜ yds.	4 yds.
Fussy cut	⅞ yd.	3 yds.	4¼ yds.	6¾ yds.	8 yds.
Print for B block corners	⅜ yd.	1¼ yds.	2 yds.	3 yds.	3¾ yds.
Inner border	¼ yd.	⅜ yd.	½ yd.	¾ yd.	¾ yd.
Middle border	¼ yd.	¼ yd.	⅜ yd.	½ yd.	½ yd.
Outer border	¾ yd.	1¼ yds.	1¾ yds.	1⅞ yds.	2⅝ yds.
Backing	1⅜ yds.	3¾ yds.	6 yds.	9 yds.	10⅛ yds.
Binding	⅜ yd.	½ yd.	⅝ yd.	¾ yd.	⅞ yd.
Batting	Crib size	Twin size	Double size	King size	King size

Cutting

	Wall/baby	Lap	Twin	Double	Queen
From 6 black-and-white or dark prints, cut:					
2½" x 21" strips	6 *total*	18 *total*	32 *total*	50 *total*	61 *total*
From 12 bright or light prints, cut:					
2½" x 21" strips	6 *total*	18 *total*	32 *total*	50 *total*	61 *total*
From print for B block centers, cut:					
8½" x 8½" squares	4	17	31	49	60
From print for B block corners, cut:					
4½" x 42" strips	2	8	14	22	27
Crosscut into 4½" x 4½" squares	16	68	124	196	240
From fabric for inner border, cut:					
1½" x 42" strips	4	5	7	–	–
2½" x 42" strips	–	–	–	8	9

From fabric for middle border, cut:					
1" x 42" strips	4	5	7	–	–
1½" x 42" strips	–	–	–	9	10
From fabric for outer border, cut:					
4½" x 42" strips	4	–	–	–	–
5½" x 42" strips	–	6	–	–	–
6½" x 42" strips	–	–	8	9	–
8½" x 42" strips	–	–	–	–	10
From fabric for binding, cut:					
2¼" x 42" strips	4	6	8	10	11

Strip Set A

	Wall/baby	Lap	Twin	Double	Queen
No. of strip sets	5	18	32	50	61
No. of 2½" segments to crosscut	40	144	256	400	488

Block Assembly

1. To make block A, with right sides together and raw edges aligned, stitch a 2½" x 21" black-and-white or dark print strip to a 2½" x 21" bright or light print strip. Press the seam allowance toward the dark fabric. Repeat with the remaining strips to make the number of strip sets indicated in the strip set A chart above. Make as many different fabric combinations as possible. Crosscut the strip sets into the number of 2½"-wide segments indicated in the chart.

2. Sew two 2½" segments together into a four-patch unit as shown. Press the seam allowance in one direction. Repeat with the remaining segments. Try to arrange the segments so each four-patch unit is made up of 4 different fabrics.

Four-patch unit

3. Arrange 4 four-patch units as shown. I try to position the fabrics so 2 squares of the same fabric do not appear too close together, but I do not obsess about it. Much. Sew the four-patch units together. Press the seam allowances as indicated. Repeat with the remaining four-patch units to complete the A blocks.

Block A

4. To make block B, mark a diagonal line from corner to corner on the wrong side of each 4½" x 4½" corner square.

5. With right sides together, place a corner square on 2 opposite corners of an 8½" x 8½" center square, matching the raw edges at the corners. Sew on the marked line. Trim the excess of the *smaller squares only*, leaving about a ¼" seam allowance. I leave the center-square fabric intact to reduce distortion. Press the triangles toward the corners of the block. Repeat with the remaining 8½" squares.

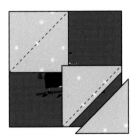

6. Repeat step 5 for the remaining 2 corners. Press the seam allowances toward the corners of the block.

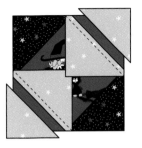

Block B

Dragon's Dance by Robin Strobel, 2001, Issaquah, Washington, 53" x 69¼".

The batik fabric used in this quilt is another print I thought would work well for the Two Blocks Are Better Than One pattern. For the alternate blocks, I chose one fabric for the dark and twelve fabrics for the lights. The corner triangles covered more of the dragons than I liked, so I put corner triangles on only two corners of each of the B blocks.

Quilt-Top Assembly

1. Refer to the quilt assembly diagram to arrange the blocks into horizontal rows, alternating the A and B blocks in each row. Take time to arrange the A blocks so the fabrics form a pleasing pattern. Sew the blocks in each row together. Press all seam allowances toward the A blocks. Sew the rows together. Press the seam allowances in one direction.

2. Refer to "Adding Borders" on page 8 to cut the border strips to size and to stitch the inner, then the middle, and finally the outer borders to the quilt top.

Quilt Finishing

1. Layer the backing, batting, and quilt top; baste the layers together.
2. Quilt as desired.
3. Bind the quilt edges.

Casual Tip

With "Crabby Witches," I found I liked the effect of using the block B corner fabric as an inner border to make the quilt center appear to float in space. Visually the inner border disappears and the thin, red middle border defines the quilt shape. It is a fun trick, but not one that will work with every quilt.

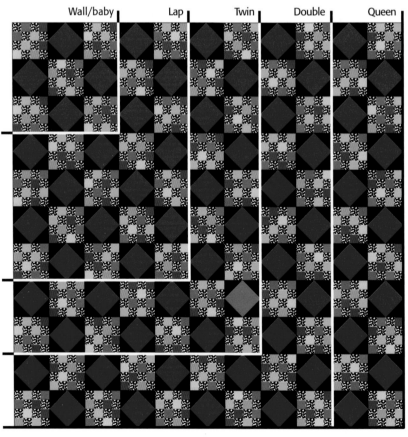

Wall/baby   Lap   Twin   Double   Queen

Quilt Assembly Diagram

Stairway to Heaven

Stairway to Heaven by Robin Strobel, 1999, Issaquah, Washington, 52" x 67".
Quilted by Rhoda Lonergan.

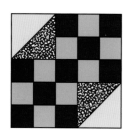 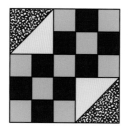

| Block A | Block B |
| Finished size: 7½" x 7½" | Finished size: 7½" x 7½" |

I named this quilt for the strong diagonal movement that is reminiscent of the traditional Jacob's Ladder design. Two checkerboard units are set diagonally so they appear to overlap. Half-square-triangle units are then added to the open corners. I confess, I did not invent the concept of overlapping blocks. Many very talented quilters, such as Mary Ellen Hopkins, Joen Wolfrom, and Judy Martin, are known for this creative design twist.

Make It Easy

- You only have to choose two light and two dark fabrics for this quilt. Light 1 and dark 1 form the half-square triangles, and light 2 and dark 2 form the checkerboard pattern.
- The size and quantity of strips required for light 2 and dark 2 are identical. You can save time by layering the two fabrics and cutting them simultaneously (see page 6).

- Try to make your ¼" seams as accurate as possible when sewing the strip sets.
- Pay attention to the light and dark orientation of the half-square triangles in block A and block B. The most common error in constructing this pattern is in positioning the triangle units.
- If you are new to quilting, make one of the smaller sizes. This is not a difficult quilt to construct, but it will take longer and be fussier than the others in this book. I love the smaller block size and the triangles in this quilt even though they are more work.
- There are many methods for constructing half-square-triangle units. Each has advantages and drawbacks. Recently I discovered a product called Triangles on a Roll, a preprinted grid for sewing half- and quarter-square-triangle units. I like how quickly I seem to be able to cut and sew large numbers of triangles from two fabrics, and the finished units are fairly accurate in size and shape. As for disadvantages, besides cost, the product is available in limited sizes, and you have the additional step of tearing the product away from the stitched triangles. Also, this method works best if you are using only two fabrics for all of the half-square-triangle units. I realize this technique is not for everyone, so I have given instructions for another method as well. It does not matter how you create half-square-triangle units as long as they are the correct size. (Your triangles can actually be approximately ⅛" off, but the more accurate they are, the easier the top will be to sew together.)

Quilt Information

	Lap	Large lap	Twin	Double	Queen
Finished size with borders	45½" x 60½"	52" x 67"	69" x 84"	79½" x 87"	89" x 104"
Blocks wide x blocks tall	5 x 7	6 x 8	8 x 10	9 x 10	10 x 12
No. of pieced A blocks	18	24	40	45	60
No. of pieced B blocks	17	24	40	45	60

Materials • 42"-wide fabric

	Lap	Large lap	Twin	Double	Queen
Light 1 for half-square-triangle units	⅝ yd.	⅞ yd.	1⅛ yds.	1⅜ yds.	1⅝ yds.
Dark 1 for half-square-triangle units	⅝ yd.	⅞ yd.	1⅛ yds.	1⅜ yds.	1⅝ yds.
Light 2 for checkerboard units	1⅛ yds.	1⅜ yds.	2⅛ yds.	2⅜ yds.	3⅛ yds.
Dark 2 for checkerboard units	1⅛ yds.	1⅜ yds.	2⅛ yds.	2⅜ yds.	3⅛ yds.
Inner border	¼ yd.	¼ yd.	⅜ yd.	½ yd.	½ yd.
Outer border	¾ yd.	⅞ yd.	1¼ yds.	1½ yds.	1⅞ yds.
Backing	3¼ yds.	3¾ yds.	4¾ yds.	5¼ yds.	9 yds.
Binding	½ yd.	½ yd.	⅝ yd.	⅝ yd.	¾ yd.
Batting	Twin size	Twin size	Double size	Queen size	King size

Cutting

	Lap	Large lap	Twin	Double	Queen
From light 1, cut:	Refer to "Block Assembly" below.				
From dark 1, cut:	Refer to "Block Assembly" below.				
From light 2, cut:					
2" x 42" strips	16	21	34	38	51
From dark 2, cut:					
2" x 42" strips	16	21	34	38	51
From fabric for inner border, cut:					
1" x 42" strips	5	6	7	–	–
1½" x 42" strips	–	–	–	8	9
From fabric for outer border, cut:					
4" x 42" strips	5	6	–	–	–
4½" x 42" strips	–	–	8	–	–
5½" x 42" strips	–	–	–	8	–
6½" x 42" strips	–	–	–	–	9
From fabric for binding, cut:					
2¼" x 42" strips	6	6	8	8	10

Block Assembly

To create the half-square-triangle units needed for this quilt, choose either the Triangles on a Roll method or the two-squares method. You will need the same number of units no matter which method you use (refer to the chart on page 42 for the number of units needed for each quilt size). If you choose the Triangles on a Roll method, you will need foundations for a 3" finished block size.

Half-square-triangle unit

Half-Square-Triangle Units

	Lap	Large lap	Twin	Double	Queen
No. of units	70	96	160	180	240

Triangles on a Roll Method

1. Refer to the cutting chart below to cut the number of strips needed. For half strips, cut the strip in half widthwise to measure 8¼" x 21". I always add ¼" to the manufacturer's suggested cut width because the fabric and paper can shift slightly.

Triangles on a Roll Cutting

	Lap	Large lap	Twin	Double	Queen
From light 1 and dark 1, cut:					
8¼" x 42" strips	2 each	2½ each	4 each	5 each	6 each

2. Place a light 1 strip and a dark 1 strip right sides together. Cut a length of Triangles on a Roll paper to fit the strip length. With the marked side face up, pin the paper to the top of the paired strips through all the layers. Place the pins in the center of the triangles.

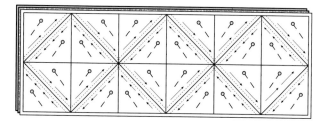

3. Shorten your stitch length so it is slightly shorter than normal. Sew along all of the dashed lines. (You do not have to follow the direction of the printed arrows, but they are helpful.) Carefully use a rotary blade and ruler to cut along the solid lines. I cut along the solid lines that separate the strips into squares first because that cut has to be the most accurate; then I cut along the solid lines that cut the squares in half diagonally. Remove the paper and press the seam allowances toward the dark fabric. Set the half-square-triangle units aside.

Casual Tip

When removing the paper, fold the paper against the seam line, then back to its original position. Place your fingernail right over the seam as you tear the paper and it will pull away from the fabric cleanly.

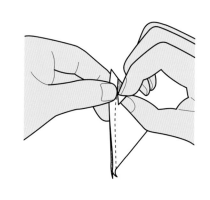

Two-Squares Cutting

	Lap	Large lap	Twin	Double	Queen
From light 1 and dark 1, cut:					
3⅞" x 42" strips	4 each	5 each	8 each	9 each	12 each
Crosscut into 3⅞" x 3⅞" squares	35 each	48 each	80 each	90 each	120 each

Two-Squares Method

1. Refer to the cutting chart above to cut the number of squares needed.
2. Draw a diagonal line from corner to corner on the wrong side of each light 1 square. I usually use a pencil.

3. Place a light 1 and a dark 1 square right sides together. With the light 1 square on top, stitch ¼" from the marked line. Try to be as accurate as possible. Chain-piece all of the squares together in this manner.

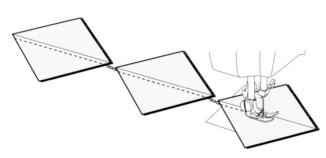

4. Without cutting the pieces apart, turn the chain-pieced squares, and stitch ¼" on the opposite side of the marked line.

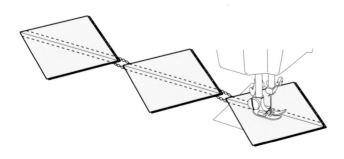

5. Cut the chain-pieced squares apart. Cut each stitched square in half diagonally along the marked line. (You do not need to be accurate.) Press the seam allowances toward the dark fabric. Once the half-square-triangle units are created, the rest of the quilt goes together quickly!

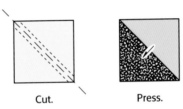

Cut.   Press.

Make the Checkerboard Units

1. With right sides together and raw edges aligned, sew a light 2 strip and a dark 2 strip together along the long edges to make strip set A. Press the seam allowance toward the dark strip. Make the number of strip sets indicated in the strip set A chart on page 45. Crosscut the strip sets into the number of 2"-wide segments indicated in the chart.

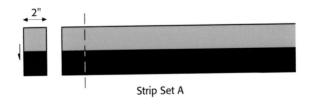

Strip Set A

2. With right sides together and raw edges aligned, sew a light 2 strip to both long edges of a dark 2 strip to make strip set B. Press the seam allowances toward the dark strip. Make the number of strip sets as indicated in the strip set B chart on page 45. For half strips, cut two 2" x 42" light 2 strips and one 2" x 42" dark 2 strip in half widthwise to measure 2" x 21". Stitch the half strips together in

the same manner as the full-length strips. Crosscut the strip sets into the number of 2"-wide segments indicated in the chart.

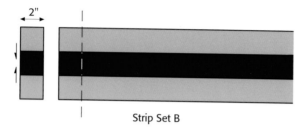

Strip Set B

3. With right sides together and raw edges aligned, sew a dark 2 strip to both long edges of a light 2 strip to make strip set C. Press the seam allowances toward the dark strip. Make the number of strip sets indicated in the strip set C chart on page 45. For half strips, cut two 2" x 42" dark 2 strips and one 2" x 42" light 2 strip in half widthwise to measure 2" x 21". Stitch the half strips together in the same manner as the full-length strips. Crosscut the strip sets into the number of 2"-wide segments indicated in the chart.

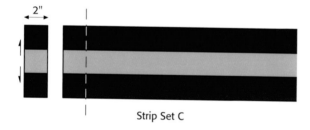

Strip Set C

4. Sew a strip set B segment to a strip set C segment as shown. Press the seam allowance toward the strip set C segment to make a six-patch unit. Refer to "Quilt Information" on page 40 to make 1 six-patch unit for each block A and block B in your quilt.

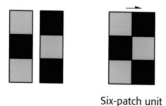

Six-patch unit

5. Sew a strip set B segment to each side of a strip set C segment as shown to make a light checkerboard unit. Press the seam allowances toward the

strip set C segment. Refer to the chart on page 45 for the number of light checkerboard units to make for each quilt size.

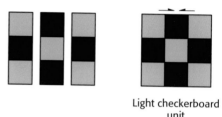

Light checkerboard unit

6. Sew a strip set C segment to each side of a strip set B segment as shown to make a dark checkerboard unit. Press the seam allowances toward the strip set C segments. Refer to the chart on page 45 for the number of dark checkerboard units to make for each quilt size.

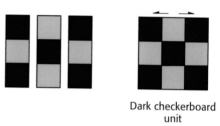

Dark checkerboard unit

Assemble the Blocks

1. Arrange 2 half-square-triangle units, 1 strip set A segment, 1 six-patch unit, and 1 dark checkerboard unit as shown to make block A. Check to be certain the light and dark squares alternate and the light triangles are on outside corners. Stitch the pieces together. Refer to "Quilt Information" on page 40 for the number of A blocks required.

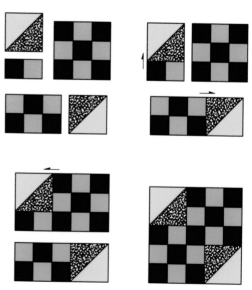

Block A

Strip Set A

	Lap	Large lap	Twin	Double	Queen
No. of strip sets	2	3	4	5	6
No. of 2" segments to crosscut	35	48	80	90	120

Strip Set B

	Lap	Large lap	Twin	Double	Queen
No. of strip sets	4½	6	10	11	15
No. of 2" segments to crosscut	87	120	200	225	300

Strip Set C

	Lap	Large lap	Twin	Double	Queen
No. of strip sets	4½	6	10	11	15
No. of 2" segments to crosscut	88	120	200	225	300

Light Checkerboard Unit

	Lap	Large lap	Twin	Double	Queen
No. of units	17	24	40	45	60

Dark Checkerboard Unit

	Lap	Large lap	Twin	Double	Queen
No. of units	18	24	40	45	60

2. Arrange 2 half-square-triangle units, 1 strip set A segment, 1 six-patch unit, and 1 light checkerboard unit as shown to make block B. Check to be certain the light and dark squares alternate and the dark triangles are on outside corners. Stitch the pieces together. Refer to "Quilt Information" on page 40 for the number of B blocks required.

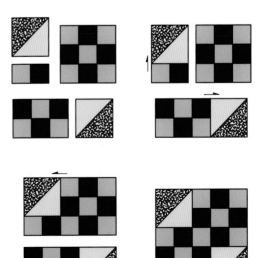

Block B

Casual Tip

It took me a while to learn how to get the points of the triangles to match. First, I don't worry too much about the width of the seam allowance on the part of a block that contains a triangle. I just make the seam allowance whatever the triangle point is.

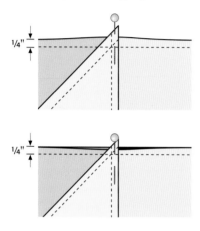

If possible, I sew with the triangle on top so I can easily see the point. Pin through the seams, making certain they match. Stitch, aiming for one thread-width past the triangle point. Remove the pin just before sewing across it. When the fabric is opened and pressed, the point will appear to be perfect.

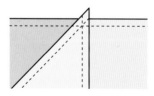

Sewing with the triangle on top is not always possible. Try this technique if the triangle falls below. Pin the fabrics together, making certain the seams match. Stab a pin straight through the tip of the triangle point, and mark the fabric on the opposite side with a pin. Stitch directly through the marked point.

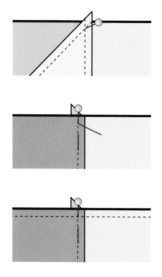

No matter how often I sew triangles, sometimes I miss sewing accurate points. When I miss, the first questions I ask are how bad does it look, and how important is it that the points be perfect? If it does not look too bad, and/or if the quilt does not need to be perfect, I leave it. Some fabric combinations show inaccuracies more than others. If I decide I want to fix it, I correct only the small area that bothers me.

There are two basic fixes. If the seams match but the seam allowance is too narrow, I simply re-stitch, taking a slightly larger bite. Remember to sew with the triangle on top!

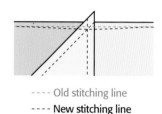

- - - - Old stitching line
- - - - **New stitching line**

If the seam allowance is too wide, and/or the seams do not match, I take out the original stitching, usually up to the last place at which a seam or point matched correctly, and pin the errant point and a few places in between. Start by overlapping the original stitching for five to six stitches and sew the section, easing and stretching as needed to get the seams and points to match. (Remove the pins just before you sew over them.) End by sewing over the original stitching for five or six stitches.

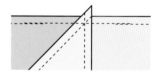

Take a look. Is it good enough? If not, take a look from about five feet away. Remember, most people are too polite to stick their noses into quilts to check all the points and seams. Are you certain it is not good enough? How about from ten feet away? From across the street?

Quilt-Top Assembly

1. Refer to the quilt assembly diagram to alternate the A and B blocks in rows. Stitch together the blocks in each row. Press the seam allowances in each row in alternate directions. Stitch the rows together. Press the seam allowances in one direction.
2. Refer to "Adding Borders" on page 8 to cut the border strips to size and to stitch the inner and then the outer borders to the quilt top.

Quilt Finishing

1. Layer the backing, batting, and quilt top; baste the layers together.
2. Quilt as desired.
3. Bind the quilt edges.

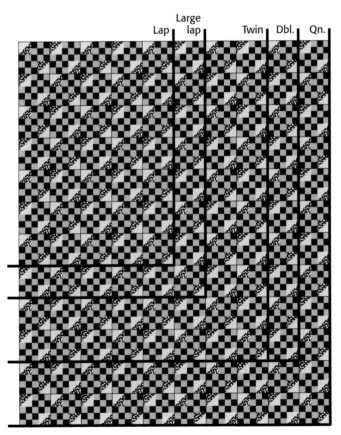

Quilt Assembly Diagram

Fish Ladder by Robin Strobel, 2001, Issaquah, Washington, 56½" x 72". Quilted by Janice Nelson.

I was at a quilt retreat on one of the San Juan Islands when I realized the fabrics I had originally selected for this quilt would not work. Though I was limited to the fabrics I had on hand, I was determined to finish this top. I generally like bright yellow-green fabrics, but only in small amounts, so it was a stretch outside my comfort zone to use one as a major player in this quilt. I grumbled, groused, and whined all through the weekend, but persevered and completed the top.

Except for the borders, the construction of this quilt is identical to that of "Stairway to Heaven" (page 39), yet it looks entirely different. The main reason for this is that the two fabrics used in the half-square triangles in this quilt both read fairly dark in value. This puts the focus on the checkerboard—the area with the most contrast.

"Fish Ladder" is not my favorite quilt, so imagine my surprise in finding that some people like it better than the other one! It just goes to show that even if you do not like a quilt you have made, it doesn't mean it is an ugly quilt. Someone, somewhere, will think it is wonderful.

About the Author

Robin Strobel enjoys living in the Pacific Northwest, where there are no fewer than twelve quilt stores reachable in an hour or less. After working in retail, in medical administration, as a veterinary technician, and as a high school science teacher, she has found her niche as an illustrator for quilting and craft books.

"I know that fabric I buy for my stash will always be a quarter-yard short when I try to use it in a project."

The Casual Quilter